Your Body:

1. Skin and Bone

Dr. Gwynne Vevers

Illustrated by Sarah Pooley

LOTHROP, LEE & SHEPARD BOOKS
New York

OTHER TITLES IN THIS SERIES
Blood and Lungs
Feeding and Digestion
Muscles and Movement

Text copyright © 1983 by Gwynne Vevers
Illustrations © 1983 by Sarah Pooley
First published in Great Britain in 1983 by The Bodley Head
Printed in the United States of America.
First U.S. Edition   1   2   3   4   5   6   7   8   9   10
Library of Congress Cataloging in Publication Data
Vevers, Gwynne, 1916-
  Your body.
  Includes index.
  Contents: 1. Skin and Bone—2. Blood and lungs— [etc.]—4. Muscles and movement.
  1. Body, Human—Juvenile literature. 2. Body, Human. I. Pooley, Sarah, ill. II. Title.
QP37.V48   1983   612   83-18757
ISBN 0-688-02820-9
ISBN 0-688-02821-7 (lib. bdg.)

Skin

Skin covers the whole human body. It is a protective and very flexible covering. Skin is waterproof, and so it not only prevents the inside parts of your body from becoming wet when you swim or take a bath, but also holds in your body fluids. Skin also keeps out germs that cause disease.

Most of the body's skin is 4–8 hundredths of an inch (1–2 mm) thick, but it is much thicker—about ⅕ inch (5 mm) thick—on the soles of your feet, and very thin where it covers your eyeballs.

Skin weighs more than these three bags of sugar!

If your skin weren't waterproof, how could you take a bath?

Skin is made up of two layers, an inner layer called the dermis and a much thinner outer layer called the epidermis.

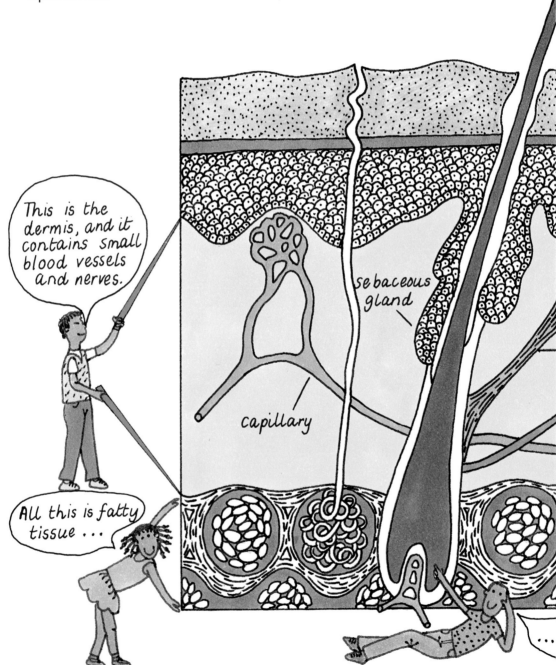

The dermis contains many small blood vessels and large numbers of long, thin, coiled tubes known as sweat glands, which keep your body temperature constant despite changes in climate.

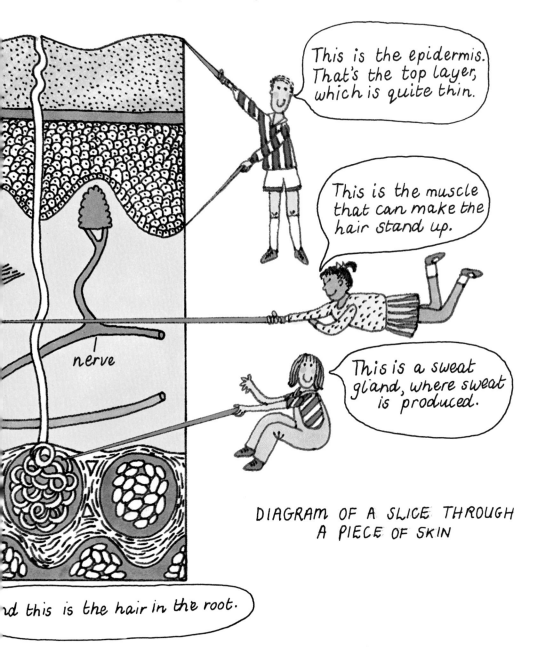

This is the epidermis. That's the top layer, which is quite thin.

This is the muscle that can make the hair stand up.

This is a sweat gland, where sweat is produced.

nerve

...d this is the hair in the root.

DIAGRAM OF A SLICE THROUGH A PIECE OF SKIN

Poor old Lucy has the flu and her temperature has gone up, so she's sweating a lot to cool her down.

These produce the watery sweat that seeps out from your body through tiny holes in the skin called pores. If you look at your skin under a magnifying glass, you will be able to see these pores. Sweat is being produced all the time, but usually it cannot be seen. However, if you become really hot, after running or when you are ill, for instance, the sweat glands produce large amounts of sweat because of the need to get rid of heat, and this can be seen as glistening drops on the surface of the skin. The sweat disappears into the air by evaporation, and your body becomes cooler again.

BODY AT NORMAL TEMPERATURE

SWEATING BEGINS TEMPERATURE RISING

CLOSE-UP OF A SWEAT GLAND

Over most parts of your body there are about 650 sweat glands in each square inch (6.45 square centimeters) of skin, but there are about four times as many as this on the palms of the hands. This is why the palms of your hands become damp and sticky when you are very hot. The soles of your feet also have very large numbers of sweat glands.

SWEAT EVAPORATES

SWEATING STOPS AS BODY RETURNS TEMPERATURE TO NORMAL

99,945
99,946
99,947
99,948...
phew!

When Mark decided to become a skinhead last week, he was completely bald, but now his hair is already 8/100 inch (2mm) long.

Most of your body, apart from the soles of your feet and the palms of your hands, is covered by hairs. These are usually quite short, but the hairs on your head grow much longer. There are between 100,000 and 200,000 hairs on the head, and each grows about 8 hundredths of an inch (2 mm) a week. Although an eyelash may last for four months, a single scalp hair may last for about four years. After this the hair is replaced by a new hair.

The dermis contains the roots of the hairs, which are called hair follicles. These are tiny pockets, each

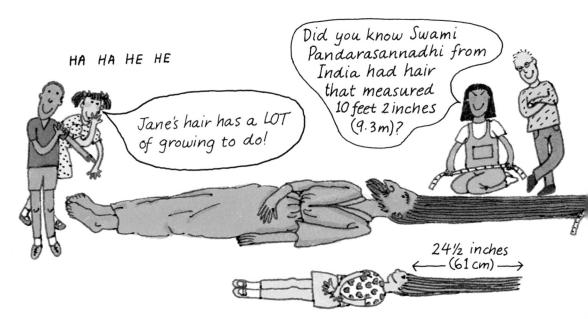

HA HA HE HE

Jane's hair has a LOT of growing to do!

Did you know Swami Pandarasannadhi from India had hair that measured 10 feet 2 inches (9.3m)?

24½ inches
← (61 cm) →

of which produces a hair and pushes it out toward the surface as a flexible but dead structure. So you don't feel any pain when your hair is cut because the parts of the hairs outside the skin are dead.

Alongside each hair follicle, there is a small muscle which can contract to make the hair stand upright. Many animals, such as cats and dogs, can make their hair stand upright when they are cold or frightened by an enemy. The erect hairs make them appear larger, and the enemy may go away. In furry animals the erect hairs trap air to form an insulating layer which keeps in the heat.

Humans can still raise their hairs to a limited extent. You can see and feel this when you are cold and have goose pimples on your arms; this can also happen when something frightens you suddenly.

Alongside each hair follicle there is another kind of gland, the sebaceous gland. It produces a greasy substance, sebum, that helps to keep the skin pliable and also oils the hair.

The dermis has large numbers of nerves which make your skin very sensitive, so that it can feel the difference between wet and dry or hot and cold. It also responds to pressure. So a gentle touch on your skin feels pleasant, but a prick with a pin is painful.

twelve noon   one o'clock

The epidermis is growing all the time, making more new skin at the bottom and pushing old skin outward. As it reaches the surface, the old skin dies, becomes scaly, and is rubbed off. So skin is being worn away all the time but in very small amounts, except when it is damaged by sunburn and the top layer peels off.

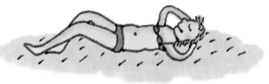

two o'clock   Later that evening

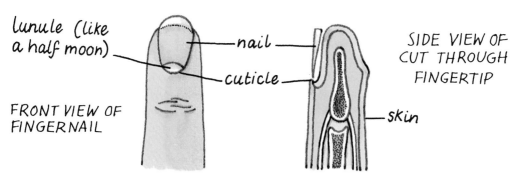

lunule (like a half moon)

nail

cuticle

FRONT VIEW OF FINGERNAIL

SIDE VIEW OF CUT THROUGH FINGERTIP

skin

At the end of each finger and toe there is a nail which is made of a hard substance called keratin. Nails go on growing from the base throughout life. Cats, dogs, and many other animals have claws made of the same substance on their front and hind paws, and birds have claws on their legs. Cows, sheep, and deer have hooves made of keratin.

Human nails grow at the average rate of about 8 hundredths of an inch (2 mm) a month, slightly more in summer than in winter. Fingernails grow about four times as fast as toenails.

Look at those nails, Mom! It would take ages to paint them!

I'm Shridhar Chillal of Poona, India, and I was born in 1937.

Shridhar achieved a measured total of 116½ inches (296 cm) for the five nails on his hand, which remained uncut since 1952.

The color of your skin is due mainly to a pigment called melanin, which may be black or various shades of brown. Pale-skinned people have very little pigment, but dark-skinned people have a lot. There is more melanin in the skin of those races whose origin is in warmer parts of the world. In places where the sun is very hot, the skin becomes tanned, which helps to protect it from being burned. Freckles are small areas of pigment that appear in some pale-skinned people.

The fingers and the palms of the hands have tiny ridges which form a pattern. These patterns are different in each person, which is why police use fingerprints to track down burglars and other criminals. Dip the tip of your finger into black shoe polish and then press it onto a piece of white paper. It will leave a fingerprint. Ask some of your friends to do the same and then compare the results.

Bone

Bone is a hard substance that makes up the skeleton, or framework, of the body, giving it shape and supporting its weight. If we didn't have bones at all, we would look like this:

There are about 200 bones of all shapes and sizes in the body of a grownup. Babies have more than 300 bones, but many of these join together as the baby grows. We need lots of small bones to enable us to move around; if we had only one large bone supporting our bodies, we would be quite rigid.

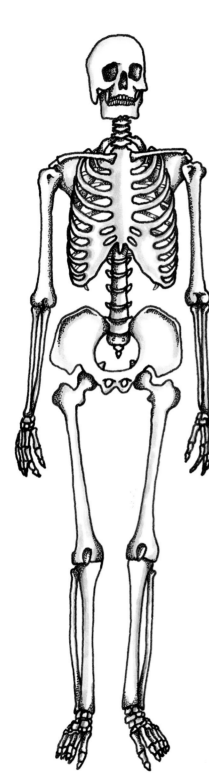

I don't believe it!

My baby sister has 100 bones more than me.

The spine, or backbone, has 33 chunky bones, known as vertebrae, which fit together, one above the other, to form a strong column. There are seven vertebrae in the neck (cervical vertebrae), twelve in the chest region (thoracic vertebrae), and five in the lower part of the back (lumbar vertebrae). The next five vertebrae are joined together, forming what is known as the sacrum, and the last four are all that remains in humans of a tail.

The spinal vertebrae are separated by pads of a springy substance called cartilage. Each vertebra is joined to the next one by ligaments, which are tough bands of a kind of fiber.

7
cervical
vertebrae

12
thoracic
vertebrae

5
lumbar
vertebrae

the
sacrum

the
coccyx

SIDE VIEW
OF SPINE

The coccyx is the human's tail.

cartilage
cartilage

THREE LUMBAR
VERTEBRAE SEEN
FROM THE SIDE

arch

rib attaches
here

hole through which
spinal cord passes

the central body

A CHEST VERTEBRA
SEEN FROM ABOVE

17

The skull is a box at the top of your spine, formed by several curved plates of bone which protect your brain. Apart from the jaws, the bones in the skull are not movable in adults.

The jaws hold your teeth. Each tooth has a crown, a neck, and a root. The crown is the hard part you can see if you look in a mirror. The neck is hidden just behind the gums, and the root is buried within the jawbone. If you count your teeth, you will find you have 20, ten in each jaw. As you grow older, these are gradually lost and replaced by the permanent

teeth you will have for the rest of your life. There are 32 of these. In each jaw there are four incisor teeth and two canine teeth. The incisors, which are the ones in the middle, are used for cutting, gnawing, and slicing when, for instance, you bite a piece of meat or bread. The teeth toward the back of the mouth are the four premolars and the six molars. These are the large teeth that grind the food when you chew.

The last two molars in each jaw are known as the wisdom teeth, and in some people these may not grow in at all.

UPPER AND
LOWER JAWS
WITH TEETH

premolar

canine

The teeth at the front of your mouth cut, gnaw, and slice.

molar

These big teeth at the back are for grinding food.

incisor

These are the roots that are embedded in the jaw.

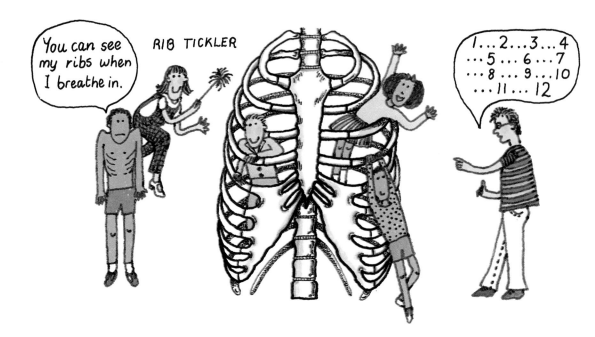

In the chest region there are twelve pairs of ribs, each joined at the back to one of the twelve thoracic vertebrae. Most of them also are attached to the breastbone (sternum) at the front. They make a cage that protects the heart and lungs. You can feel your ribs quite easily at the side of your chest.

In the shoulder region there is a girdle made of two bones, the collarbone (clavicle) in front and the shoulder blade (scapula) at the back of the chest. You can feel the clavicle on each side of your neck.

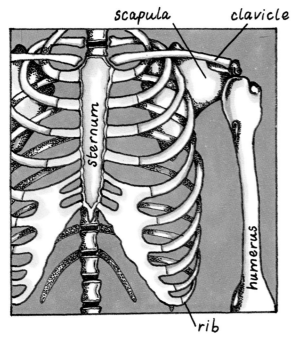

scapula   clavicle

sternum

humerus

rib

The bone of your upper arm, called the humerus, has a knob at the top which fits into a pit in the shoulder blade to form a joint which is movable. If you keep one arm straight and swing it around in a circle, you will understand how this upper arm joint allows a great amount of movement in all directions.

Your lower arm, between the elbow and the wrist, has two bones which are called the radius and the ulna. They join the humerus at the elbow, and they carry the wrist and finger bones at their lower end. If you hold your arm out with the palm of the hand upward, the radius is the bone on the outside or thumb side. The ulna is on the other side of the arm, and both bones can be felt easily.

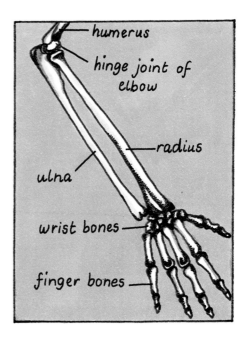

humerus

hinge joint of elbow

radius

ulna

wrist bones

finger bones

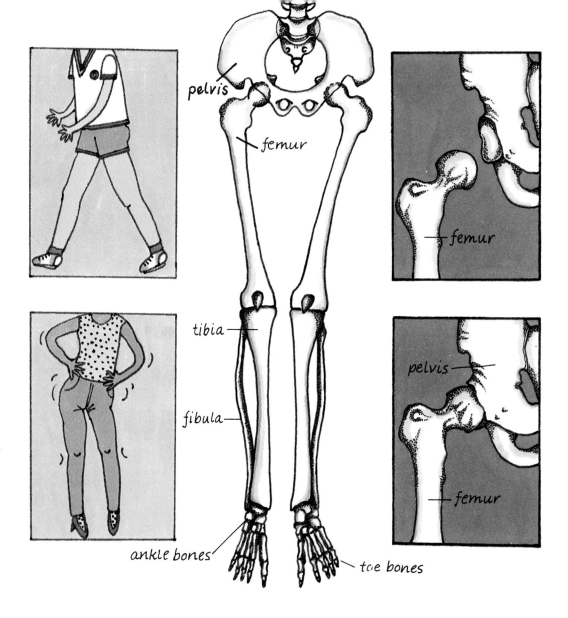

pelvis

femur

femur

tibia

pelvis

fibula

femur

ankle bones

toe bones

In the hip region there is a large, strong, bony arch, the pelvis, connected to the sacrum. Each long thighbone, called the femur, has a large knob at the upper end that fits into a pit in the pelvis. This gives a strong hip joint that allows you to move your legs around, not only backward and forward, but also from side to side.

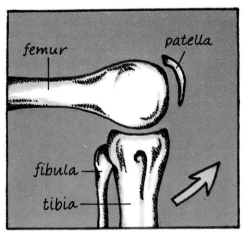

KNEE JOINT SEEN FROM THE SIDE

The lower end of the femur is joined to the bones below at the knee. The lower part of your leg, between the knee joint and the ankle, has two bones which are called the tibia and the fibula. They carry the ankle and toe bones at their lower end. You can feel the tibia, the shinbone, at the front of your lower leg. The fibula is the very thin bone alongside it.

The knee joint has a cap, called the patella, and works like a hinge. It is open when you stand up and fully closed when you squat on your heels on the floor. The hinge also opens and closes when you run.

23

Index

Page numbers in *italic type* indicate illustrations.